Secrets to make a living from cryptocurrencies

Content

How much money it takes to make a living from cryptocurrencies 5

Reasons to invest in cryptocurrencies 10

Discover the profitability of a lifetime of Bitcoin trading 13

Real testimonial on how to make a living from Bitcoin investments 19

Ambitions to make a living from trading 23

How much must you generate to make a living from cryptocurrency? 30

Some recommendations for making a living from cryptocurrencies 34

General experiences of living off cryptocurrencies 38

Ways to save and live off cryptocurrencies 39

The skills to make a living from cryptocurrency trading 43

The regular salary of the crypto world 49

Retirement savings in cryptocurrencies 53

Buying cryptocurrencies as collateral on the road to retirement 55

Retirement plans designed based on cryptocurrencies 57

Launching Bitwage to create a retirement plan 63

The best cryptocurrencies for creating a pension plan 67

Cryptoassets as a sign of the future for pension funds 69

Actions to avoid in order to make a living from cryptocurrencies 72

The generation of income with technological advances has diversified completely, where an interesting option stands out in the short, medium and long term, such as cryptocurrencies, but there are still some doubts about how to turn this means into a source of income that allows you to live comfortably.

Behind some cryptocurrencies lies the key to lessening your financial worries, but it is still a risk in itself as it is an investment and like any other, there is the possibility of making or losing money, but by dealing with that outcome you are going to be able to be open to significant gains.

How much money it takes to make a living from cryptocurrencies

When you are thinking of investing in cryptocurrencies, a detail that you must estimate is the type of capital that you must have to multiply the figures in positive earnings, there are different ways or modalities to achieve this type of economic result, as you can learn about this world you can dedicate what is necessary.

From the beginning you must keep a realistic view of the risks you face, as well as the aspects of this economic world, different managers use their knowledge to participate in cryptocurrency investments, and an important point to discuss is how you can invest.

- **Choosing hodler or cryptotrader**

At the moment of being part of the investment of cryptocurrencies you can adopt two types of modalities, these depend on the type of time that you have to dedicate to this activity, as well as the magnitude of the capital destined for this investment, therefore this is classified in two ways.

Firstly, you have the option of obtaining an optimal level of profit to the point of living off this investment, and on the other hand there are also participants who only seek to achieve a level of profitability of the money you manage and this is no longer provided by a bank or a traditional entity, much less in the face of inflation.

These two concepts can be realized by means of a hodler or cryptotrader, in the case of hodlers refers to the action of holding cryptocurrencies, this alternative has the advantage that the type of capital is flexible because in the long run it will pay off.

1. **Hodler**

But before the option of hodl you must carry out an account that is totally realistic, you can start under the study of the market, as well as keeping the position of retaining and selling the assets at the best time for each step, this is a key point because otherwise there will be no profitability.

Another type of estimation that you should make is to manage the proportion of profits with respect to the investment that you are making, since if you use a capital of $1,000 USD you cannot have the expectation of generating $10,000 USD, it is rather to bet on a return that is approximately 20% or 50%, this depends on your decisions.

In case you want to live completely from cryptocurrencies, when hodling you must have an important capital, in that way you can perceive some economic benefits necessary to live, at the same time from those profits you must start to decrease everything related to taxes and others.

The issue of taxes should not be overlooked, since in countries such as Spain for example, an income or charge is established on the profit produced, about 18-21% is dedicated to the payment of such legal taxation, this is an obstacle to observe cryptocurrencies as a solution for life at a financial level.

To make a full living from a cryptocurrency investment in the hold mode, you must involve at least a capital of around $100,000 USD, but when you are only looking to generate some kind of interest through cryptocurrencies, it is best to hold and sell progressively over the long term.

However, the risk of an asset going down in price is a condition you have to deal with, these are investments that cannot be controlled, but at the same time represent a financial victory when you get it right.

- **Method for investing in cryptocurrencies**

One of the most commonly used techniques for long-term investment in cryptocurrencies is to follow the moving average, at least for a period of 120 to 150 periods, so that when the price is increasing and is around the average, or is the long-term average, the time to buy is limited.

On the other hand, there is the issue of stop loss, although different opinions classify it as a dangerous resource, especially when you are betting on a hodling position is not the most advisable, it is essential that you take care of the investment of your capital on any mode, especially in a single asset, better diversify.

2. **Cryptotrading**

Secondly, there is the position and work of cryptotrading, this is a method in which you can get more income, but at the same time to live on these results you must have a considerable amount of capital, experts recommend that you can have at least $10,000 USD.

If you are still a novice in this type of investments, do not start investing with an exaggeratedly high capital, you can practice with a much lower measure than the one mentioned above, until you create an investment plan where you can add some techniques or cryptotrading steps that are studied and tested.

As you are employing a step that works, you are going to be able to progressively move up to the point that if you are good you are going to make a living from this without any problem, but the duty is on the acquisition of knowledge, you are going to need to read and be informed in any instance to get ideas from your analysis.

No matter what you may read or research, the line you must keep is that of self-knowledge, your own determination is what will help you make the decisions you consider appropriate, especially because the limits must be set by you, that is the way to establish a personal system.

For example, if you are a hodler, you don't have to spend so much time on the operations, but in the case of a cryptotrader it is an investment of at least 4 hours a day, it all depends on the disposition you have when investing.

Reasons to invest in cryptocurrencies

When thinking about investing in cryptocurrencies to change your life and you still have doubts, you can take into account the following points to do your best, keeping the necessary conviction to achieve profits:

- Cryptocurrencies have a considerable track record, as they have been part of the financial landscape for more than 11 years and are more relevant than ever under the impetus of digital transformation.
- Given the enormous variety and quantity of assets, it is easy for you to be able to diversify your invested capital.

- On the other hand, the cost of trading these assets is very low, since modern Exchanges impose little or no commissions.
- It is currently the most reliable way to protect your capital in the face of inflation.
- Privacy is guaranteed, since the management of operations can be carried out anonymously and has nothing to do with traditional banking.
- You gain real control of your assets, observing any changes and with the possibility of withdrawing and depositing at will.
- The transfer of money is carried out in a fast and cost-effective way because it is a digital process.
- Cryptocurrencies can be used anywhere in the world, their global scale allows you to use or dispose of the asset with total freedom.
- There is no need to pay to keep money, much less when buying and selling cryptocurrencies.
- As time goes by, different facilities are being put in place to make cryptocurrencies available to you on a daily basis by means of a simple click.
- These assets are a solution to put aside the ravages of inflation.

- If you own a business, you can accept cryptocurrencies to acquire a larger number of customers.
- Little by little, some protection regulation on cryptocurrency operations is beginning to be generated, this is an important point to operate with greater confidence.
- At the beginning as a beginner you do not need a large amount of capital, you can start by getting to know all the resources that this type of investment provides.
- Following the excessive use of cryptocurrencies, more forms of investment are emerging, where yield funds and others stand out.
- The cryptocurrency world is controlled by the community, which means that no government has any kind of intervention.
- This type of investment is exciting, it can become a lifestyle for you, as different communities live this experience to the fullest.

Learning to make a living from cryptocurrencies requires above all motivation, so these reasons above are the best way to get clarity when making a decision and bet everything to improve your skills.

Discover the profitability of a lifetime of Bitcoin trading

When thinking about investing in Bitcoin trading, you must answer some previous doubts to take solid steps, since after every day is an option that has gained popularity in the long term, especially for the kind of privileges that this investment represents for many people this has been supported by the options available online.

The participation of retailers within cryptocurrencies is more accurate because of the type of facilities it grants over different areas, this is what causes that more and more people can facilitate in this section of investments, it is not that it is easy to earn, but it is profitable as you gain experience.

The practice is an element that cannot be missing in the world of cryptocurrencies, since it generates unlimited possibilities to obtain income, the purchase of an asset is simple and at the same time it works as a protection on your patrimony to avoid inflation, but you can go further and speculate to make a living from this activity.

Through some small movements and according to the market movements you can earn money, that by being a constant or performing it with a large capital you will be able to reach an optimal source of income, where the Bitcoin is an opportune option if you consider living from this type of efforts.

Before thinking of submitting yourself to this activity, the main thing is that you can believe in yourself, and not take for granted that it is an easy activity, because profitability can be assigned with progress and those actions that little by little give shape to these long-term investments.

- **Alternative holding, trading of Bitcoin and some cryptocurrencies**

The medium of cryptocurrency investments is a proliferation online, to the point that you will find special courses and trainings on this subject, since anyone wants to make a living from trading, especially since at one point it becomes an attractive measure by speculating progressively.

But in order to make profits it is vital to master certain concepts such as scalping, entry and swing trading, these terms are essential to measure the profitability of your actions, especially when you want this to be your means of income or livelihood, the duty lies on constant training.

As long as you can expose yourself to risk with better reasoning, and regardless of the type of result that is presented you should not lose the value of tolerance, this is the challenge that every type of beginner trader must face because the market can not be controlled and much less the type of setback that is presented.

Through the operations you carry out, the limit or breaking point is higher, that is what allows you to make better decisions, without worries ruling your steps, that way you can build a valuable capital in a shorter period of time, especially because you must learn to deal with high risks in order to grow profits.

The key to making a living from trading is the creation of a plan, which you will follow with a special investment of energy that possesses consistency, control of your thoughts, and also discipline, all these are points to deepen, also in some moments of the market it is vital to master the holding of cryptocurrencies.

Before you want to take risks that will propel you toward potential gains, you can take control of your actions by understanding these actions:

- **What's behind the cryptocurrency holding company**

There is no doubt that this type of cryptocurrency has to do with the way in which it is bought within this market, but it has a great distinction over trading, since it is a medium and long term investment, as a way in which this activity is understood under a slightly more leisurely pace.

This scenario is more relaxed to make decisions because you are not under so much pressure, but this does not mean that preferring trading is a negative activity, but it demands more experience not to reach a high margin of loss, as you possess knowledge you will have in your hands significant results.

The active trading requires a significant number of hours, by fulfilling this requirement is that you will get profits based on each hour and movement made, but the recommendation is to master each of these issues to dabble on the most effective way to think about long-term investment.

- **The trading plan and the psychology involved**

What matters most is the interest that you dedicate at the time of starting in the world of trading, starting by researching many details about Bitcoin, so you can find the facilities of this medium, where the first step is to build a trading plan so you have some basic rules about the exit and entry to the market.

On risk management is the opportunity to decrease the kind of losses you can face, that is an ideal way to increase success to the point of living from this investment, beyond not having the best strategy in the cryptocurrency world, but there are some golden rules to follow so that the gains outweigh the losses.

It is enough to take some premises so that when mistakes arise, you will get peace of mind, otherwise you will make hasty decisions based on your emotions, at this point the psychology that is part of the investor, which can be built through experience, enters into controversy.

But some elements that complement a good decision making, you need discipline and constancy this is what allows you to have a compliance to the letter of your strategy, but with the awareness that it is not something you can achieve from one moment to another, but everything goes hand in hand with practice to move forward.

- **Broker preference, use of demo accounts and the move to a live account**

Once you are ready to be part of the cryptocurrency investment world, the next thing is about choosing a website for trading as well as investing in cryptocurrency, but you should focus on one that you can trust and that has the best features for your investment plans.

Choosing a broker should not be classified as an easy step or a light decision, you need to make sure that it is a legal and regulated site, in addition to providing good customer service without high commissions or much less, the same goes for all the details regarding deposit and withdrawal to be convenient for your case.

Research as prevention is the best alternative to make an appropriate decision, one of the most used recommendations is Binance, since it is an interesting Exchange that is positioning itself worldwide, the offer of this portal is important to be part of the cryptocurrency movement.

Setting up a real account allows you to carry out all types of operations, from each option you can start testing your emotions until your decisions lead you to profits, regardless of whether you start with little or large capital, the important thing is to master the erratic impulse based on your emotions.

Trading with Bitcoin or any other cryptocurrency is conceived as a risky activity, but in the same way it provides important possibilities to increase your capital, so you should evaluate a management and administration of the same so that you can succeed in this investment.

Real testimonial on how to make a living from Bitcoin investments

There is no doubt that throughout the world Bitcoin has established itself as an accepted means of payment in every trade and location, everything is open or available when it comes to Bitcoin, it is also a much more profitable asset than gold, this has changed over time to put cryptocurrencies in a better place.

The Bitcoin alternative is gaining more and more strength and those who started with this asset are living a unique dream, since you can not only live through this asset but also facilitate any trip instead of moving with cash, this first cryptocurrency has been the funding point for many adventures.

The formation of the cryptocurrency ecosystem has started through Bitcoin, but to reach real profits you must live with the risk, this is a point that can be complex for many, but there are real testimonies of many users who give up and live only with Bitcoin.

In the case of the popular Didi Taihuttu, he recovered from a family loss to build his own business, but over time he adopted a materialistic vision that was challenged by another family event that took him away from business, so he had to take a break to organize his ideas.

During the trips made by this character, he began to observe the change and productivity of his assets in Bitcoin and Doge, which generated a revolution on his financial vision as good business sense drove him to be part of this option to contribute to the change in the world generated by cryptocurrencies.

At the beginning Didi Taihuttu relates that his family did not take this decision in the best way, as they were selling their properties to buy Bitcoin, but at least they agreed that they needed a less materialistic life change, that change over their lives they were betting on Bitcoin.

The full bet on Bitcoin was a reality, using the ease of buying a large amount of Bitcoin safely and quickly, everything is simple to start managing this asset, but the advantage is to go to a site where they do not accept this type of asset.

Exploring the crypto world caused him to be able to find projects to add partners, plus there is a collaboration of this payment tool to use as a means of liquidity, and many people question him on how he has survived in the face of the volatile level and falls that Bitcoin has suffered.

The answer to that scenario is to get used to the fluctuations, without thinking about it dropping to 0 because you would be bankrupt, but life is about adventures and protection lies from buying Bitcoin low, so that in the face of any movement you have a margin of profit and protection to appeal to.

Trading can be the source of income for any type of family, but in the face of downturns you should only let yourself go with the trend itself, without losing sight of all that you have earned instead of just focusing on the material, as this calms your thoughts to have a better posture to any financial turbulence.

If you have money to live on a monthly basis, there is no need to worry about the long term, within the investments comes into play the mentality, and in the end life passes with speed so it is better to enjoy the present without worrying about what happens tomorrow, you just have to hold on to the initial prediction of the price of Bitcoin that convinced you.

Each bull or bear market has its own opportunity, and on each cryptocurrency there is a historical maximum, but such movements do not arise immediately, but it all depends on the macroeconomics, as well as a lot of factors or variables, but what you should not lose faith in the chosen cryptocurrency.

The bet on Bitcoin is due to the fact that no other company or business idea has been able to sustain itself for more than 11 years, 24 hours a day, and permanently 7 days a week without an error, this is only offered by a cryptocurrency such as the pioneer project of Bitcoin.

The path of BTC still has many details to be studied, but it is undoubtedly a practice to be promoted, since it is a natural way to continue in the economic dynamics without suffering the crashes of traditional systems that occur worldwide, so cryptocurrencies are a decentralized way out.

Faced with the intention of governments to limit the flow of cash, you can opt for digital assets, this form of payment is the one that is gaining strength today, and without losing the level of privacy of these digital media, such power is part of each of the assets as DASH, BTC, and others.

The important thing is that this character reaffirms the usefulness of using any cryptocurrency of your choice, and in situations such as a pandemic there is no negative effect on these assets because they are everywhere in the world, and contrary to popular belief, their use has increased significantly.

There is no doubt that it is interesting to live on cryptocurrencies or reduce your wealth towards this asset, it is a permanent industry that you have at your disposal to obtain full peace of mind, but without missing out on what is important to live, instead of just visualizing the changes in the price.

Ambitions to make a living from trading

There is no doubt that trading is not easy, but it is a dream and a goal for many to make a living from this activity, in a situation like the Covid-19 pandemic with so many negative social, financial, health and other consequences, but it diversifies the way investors operate.

But after different broker analysis, strong results are generated that impose the preference on this type of investments for their constant availability regardless of external circumstances, but any movement can cause a state of alarm on your invested assets.

Some changes or advice are extended to overcome the pandemic phase without this activity declining, regardless of whether the reality has completely changed, the important thing is to overcome the economic crises postulated by COVID, since this is a factor that affects a large number of traditional workers.

By working from home remotely, you can solve your economic problems through a technical and tactical study, that allows you to use the security protocols to invest with greater freedom or opportunity, also in a contingency you can concentrate to work on this investment action.

The difference of working remotely has been revealed by the confinement, because the office is moved to the home and in the state of alarm the most convenient thing to do is to increase the type of operation you exercise when investing in cryptocurrencies, thus opening an account on platforms such as brokers can open the way to generate income.

The current situation or dealings with cryptocurrencies is much greater than in previous years, after each broker there is a statistic of the change or participation of each year, where the following points of study stand out:

1. **Interest in trading cryptocurrencies**

The reasons why more and more people are betting on the world of cryptocurrencies, are due to wanting to seek an economic access like this that is producing significant financial results in terms of scalability and profitability, since 2019 there have been very striking liquidity positions.

Although the year 2020 saw significant declines in the most solid assets, positions then resumed thanks to the fact that many investors took advantage of this market window to buy at low prices, and through short positions many investors were able to increase their income.

On the other hand, the push of the pandemic that limited jobs caused many incomes to begin to fade, so to combat this discouragement they bet on financial freedom online hand in hand with cryptocurrencies, which leads to comply with some investments to exercise a day-trading.

These two streams of users seeking to live from trading, do not face a simple scenario, but if really promising, it is achievable when you can strive more than most to produce income, so every day more and more people are looking to invest and get an account to operate freely.

2. **Preference for trading and strategizing on cryptocurrencies**

The changes within the markets is a usual panorama, based on the clients that are part of different brokers, it can be noticed how there are variables about their behavior, keeping two clear ideas about investing by predictions and European or North American projects, since they are the most potential in the last years.

But since 2021 the whole focus of investment in cryptocurrencies is centered on those that are backed in the world of technology, since the pandemic is a point of attraction of interest on this type of market, as well as the one that represents video games, without leaving aside the social networks.

Funds and assets have become a wide world of opportunities and possibilities to make a living from it, as long as you sustain strategies or experience within that medium, since for some it was a totally unthinkable way to live but the amount of operations shows the degree of interest.

The quotation behind each market is striking, therefore, it is a good offer to sustain a salary and live from this activity, it is an attraction and a robust side that does not seem to change, the essential thing is to dedicate yourself to the market trends, because this helps you to have a progress in your life and especially at a financial level.

When the fight against inflation is mentioned, you must immediately take into account all that cryptocurrencies represent, it is a seduction that is present in every social network you visit and it is inevitable to ignore it, especially when some great rise arises and some testimonies of gains from this movement are published.

The statements of important figures such as Elon Musk, have meant an affirmation for this investment medium to gain more strength, there are many factors of great relevance behind this world.

3. **The level of training is essential for access to this medium.**

In the midst of the platforms that allow trading with cryptocurrencies, it has become evident that new users have more knowledge, that is, there is a concern to be part of this environment and above all to generate income, new traders take their training seriously and you can not be the exception.

Taking courses or training programs is a real opportunity for you to make a living from cryptocurrency investing, but some with minimal levels or a notion of the market can get involved with investing to generate income and reinvest it in capital as well as training for yourself.

Operating on your own entails a futuristic vision to watch over your growth possibilities, this is a path to financial freedom where decisions weigh, it is a clear desire the option to live from these investments, but it is achieved only by appealing to the dedication so you can start with more than just basic concepts.

What you must learn is to use the external factor in your favor, such as researching some events or launches of important corporations or projects that are behind some cryptocurrency, this gives you an advantage so that your capital acquires a greater possibility of growth.

On the other hand, this medium forces you to live with the research of the most convenient changes, since operating with a deposit or withdrawal mode that is not favorable or that is exposed to inflation is a start that places you in a bad position, therefore your portfolio must be covered from the beginning to this variable.

The most common bet is to attend seminars that support the first steps of investment on cryptocurrencies, it is a help for you to develop a simple vision but to obtain preparation so that you have a base of fundamental analysis at least, without leaving aside the follow-up to be done on the financial world.

Online you can also find a great amount of indicators, those data are the ones that will allow you to face volatility, which is a risk that you have to get used to and can end with any kind of strategies you are designing and therefore have a direct impact on your finances.

The filter to discern which publications are valuable or not is in your hands, it is part of that power to follow official or reliable sources, the objective is that you get to know the indicators that professional investors follow and the type of effect they have on the generation of income.

The help you can get from the media is positive, especially when you create an investment strategy, without leaving aside the access to trainings that dominate this field so that you can follow more concrete steps and develop a lifestyle sponsored by the cryptocurrencies themselves, the essential thing is to keep working.

How much must you generate to make a living from cryptocurrency?

Living off the income from cryptocurrencies is a type of profitability that requires first of all knowledge, intelligence, freedom to make decisions, self-control, creativity and above all aspiration for productivity, starting from these basic measures, the next step is to set objectives or goals.

A goal has to do directly with the type of monthly income that you are able to generate, because it must be above your expenses, in addition to being worthy enough to live, and turn the investment activity into a stable and constant point, that way you can obtain passive and residual income without having to work.

With the rise of cryptocurrencies, especially the pioneer Bitcoin, there has been a common behavior of wanting to establish an income, but to reach that result you must have some support bases such as a monthly income, this helps you to extend your financial assets, especially at the beginning.

In the same way, some actions are being developed in the market where the aim is that your Bitcoins can be profitable, over and above waiting for their revaluation, because in the blockchain environment there is still a lot to exploit when it comes to generating income to live on them.

Every digital nomad is currently focused on generating their own income based on cryptocurrencies, but without creating this obstacle or waiting for a quote, but rather with certain alternatives, for example, a point of analysis is that if you own at least 2 bitcoins you can have an income of at least 6% annually.

This type or income generation is above any business such as renting an apartment, but getting to that point is a sum of steps where you can not fail to learn to thoroughly understand this market, as it has a dynamic operation where collateral instruments are applied and there are always risks.

Instead of just getting in and out of an investment, you can visualize currencies as a valuable asset, regardless of whether the project or its capitalization goes ahead or not, the essential thing is to have the conviction of the way in which you are going to survive in this environment, you must know more details about the following points:

- **The background of Bitcoin**

Several investors who thought they could make a living from Bitcoin had to overcome different difficulties, to the point of selling every element or property of their wealth to invest it entirely in this cryptocurrency, which classifies them as true digital nomads because they became to have a simpler lifestyle as a result of this financial decision.

That kind of position demands not to look or obsess about the future, but to think about a much simpler lifestyle with a more daily approach, it is time to take a break and go places, this will allow them to save bitcoins and at the same time go on with their lives.

With just a motor home and a travel group, this type of daring people undertook a different lifestyle, without touching the issue of any depression due to Bitcoin falls or much less, this lifestyle allowed many users to overcome some kind of inflation that their country was going through.

The best thing is that you keep a lifestyle that does not escalate expenses, because with cryptocurrencies you can have a much more ambitious vision and raise expenses, when in fact it is a way of generating income that needs patience and time so that your money can multiply.

Also, the upside is that you are breaking away from the system to work for you and for you, the first few months can be complex and it is feasible to use a traditional monthly income, but then you must take the big step to only using cryptocurrencies and cryptocurrency based strategies, up to using crypto financial products.

The commercial acceptance of cryptocurrencies also helps a lot so that you do not have to make an excessive change, but this generally translates into a life full of bets, although to generate great wealth you must be willing to gamble everything on your idea and be willing to live with the idea of losing.

Being at that level of risk, causes in many people that money does not have the same value for them, because the willingness to lose everything for a better future, helps you not to care too much or make hasty decisions, without thinking about what will come in the future because it is complicated to answer it.

It is a very slow journey where you know your limits, but it is also an alternative to peel for charity and use both free time and money in a much more useful destination, the possibility of being a digital nomad is behind the investor's mettle, because there are many ways to generate income and live off these assets.

Some recommendations for making a living from cryptocurrencies

The use of cryptocurrencies is taking over more regions of the world, it is a phenomenon used to confront economic crises, without forgetting that it is a stable means to withstand some havoc as in the case of a pandemic, since everything is managed digitally and is an advantage not to be overlooked or dismissed.

Digital payments are the trend of the moment, but they are financial issues to investigate and consult extensively, so you can get to get the profits you expect, with some tips you can adapt to this financial front that represents a risk or challenge for anyone, but with great rewards in between.

Cryptoassets occupied by users exceed 50% of the broker, thanks to the fact that it is observed as a means of investment to generate income, this also has to do with the changes postulated by each asset, as some results mark an increase in this investment trend.

Like any type of investment, there are some risks to live with in order to dare to make transactions with these digital assets, since cryptocurrencies require a significant level of education or training, especially to face the peak moment of operating and recognizing the regulations of this medium.

To be part of this volatile environment you should take into account the following recommendations to bet in the best way for digital currencies:

1. **Be wary of promises of exaggerated profits.**

Avoiding or ignoring some recommendations is beneficial because they may promise you too much, and in the end it is a total fraud, this is because various platforms issue huge promises in exchange for a small investment in assets of the likes of Bitcoin, Ethereum and also on Binance Coin.

The recovery of your initial investment with quick profits is not something that happens out of the blue, it is best to follow experts before making any investment based on advice, without leaving aside that this type of assets represent a much more productive option in the long term, to take advantage of market opportunities.

On the other hand, paying attention to simple users who create an account on cryptocurrencies can make you fall into a risk of being scammed, that is why many times they promise you ideal businesses based on cryptocurrencies, but they are a scam that do not double your earnings, but only want to get paid for false recommendations.

2. **Do not expose all your resources**

When you have the possibility of investing in cryptocurrencies, do not hesitate to do so in order to learn about this type of market until you discover everything it has to offer, but if you have limited savings and want to invest in cryptocurrencies, you must accept beforehand that you will live with anxiety due to the type of fluctuations that the price of this asset goes through.

The cryptocurrency landscape is under an absolute dependence on speculation as well as the degree of volatility, therefore the most appropriate is to appeal for a diversified investment because that way you can get a safer investment, while other daily face a much higher risk.

It is essential that you do not allocate all the money you are not willing to lose, so you should not allocate 100% of your capital for this purpose, since the financial impacts are uncontrollable, besides it will be an emotional condition that will not allow you to make good decisions, increasing the possibility of a terrible result.

3. **You have no legal protection**

This type of virtual trading does not have legal support, therefore the decision to be part of this world, involves accepting this idea to be aware that this situation is a risk on top of being a highly volatile market, so to take the appropriate steps it is vital to have knowledge about this medium.

Cryptocurrencies demand a considerable dedication of time, since in full time that chain of efforts is what generates profits, especially to learn to keep calm and get up in the face of a setback without losing all the time.

4. **Study in advance the promotion behind each cryptocurrency**

Instead of investing blindly in cryptocurrencies, you should take into account every detail of the same, especially because some websites place malicious content only to attract people, in the same way you should take care of your financial data, as it is a sensitive type of information that you should not share.

Before any decision you can read the comments, while investigating every aspect that generates intrigue both the company and the cryptocurrency, so you can avoid falling into any scam, in the search engine you can enter some key searches such as complaints or others to help you measure their reputation.

There is no doubt that the topic of cryptocurrencies is growing and gaining strength because of the potential gains, but it is difficult to determine whether in your case it is good or not to invest, since it is a market constantly exposed to uncertainty, but many exchange platforms are producing agreements with traditional banks.

General experiences of living off cryptocurrencies

Behind the different types of modern lifestyles, there are businesses of all kinds based on the digital era, such as paid posts and others, which become the livelihood of many families, as part of an unimaginable result of part of the digital transformation.

But a favorite form of payment among online job lovers is through cryptocurrencies, it is a common situation faced by a large number of users, in Latin countries this is an ideal alternative because it helps to survive from any kind of inflation that is present.

The profits and savings are used to be converted into cryptocurrencies in order to survive and overcome the economic complexities, therefore the experiences as a means of payment have been really positive, they have a universal use, for several years cryptocurrencies have been consolidated.

At certain points it can be thought or determined that the level of knowledge is still behind, especially because it is a market with high demands for you to use your money properly about cryptocurrencies, any doubts should be resolved in advance.

Ways to save and live off cryptocurrencies

Beyond any statistics, nowadays it is regular and frequent to buy, save and above all live on cryptocurrencies, it is part of the digital reality that we are living and little by little it has spread worldwide, both individuals and organizations are betting on mobilizing and trading with cryptocurrencies.

The ecosystem of payments with cryptocurrencies can be associated even with the payment of bonuses for employees, this generates a very important global effect in large countries such as Spain and the United States, but at the same time this level of use leads to the emergence of taxes, as a novel economic movement.

The modern cryptocurrency system allows to live through the value of this asset, to buy and even to save, it is a reality that makes sense on many testimonies, it also gives rise to other alternative services such as cryptocurrency custody to safeguard this type of investment, since it is a permitted activity.

The alternatives to take care of your earnings or patrimony are varied, this is a sample of the expansion that this medium is obtaining, where in addition to everything you must obtain a reliable gateway between crypto and fiat, within the Exchange is that you can obtain the function of spending, saving and even lending, thanks to the acceptance of this asset.

In the same way this type of possession allows you to entertain yourself and acquire everything you need, the important thing is that you can use cryptocurrencies for everything you want so it is a type of investment that you have at your fingertips to exit and enter when you see fit, this is due to the accelerated pace at which cryptocurrencies move.

Today's ATM management allows you to make transactions with cryptocurrencies, this is part of the global options that you can carry out with cryptocurrencies, under a large number of providers that buy and sell bitcoins to provide cash.

- **Buy cryptocurrency to save and live**

The financing of your lifestyle depends not only on art, but also on obtaining liabilities and assets, that is why cryptocurrencies can provide you with this alternative by just borrowing so you can start investing, trading and spending, also if you do not want to acquire so much knowledge or get involved in this medium you can be a lender.

It is a fact that cryptocurrencies provide different modalities to live and save thanks to these assets, where you must also include the influence of staking to keep the funds by means of a wallet so that the assets are in constant income production.

All these types of processes may be new for many, it is also true that there is a high level of risk and legal loopholes that could disadvantage you in case of any error or mistake, so every action requires care and extreme vigilance when operating or executing transactions.

But compared to the traditional financial system, this infrastructure increases your chances of generating a higher level of income, but above all to have the freedom of choice, while with conventional currencies you are exposed to inflation due to recurring crises worldwide.

The world of cryptocurrencies is an active ecosystem, but at the same time it depends on small details, it is a step towards a lot of novel options, but there is no doubt that it is a reality to live and save by virtue of cryptocurrencies, it is an industry that lives in evolution after evolution.

Digital transformation is advancing to bring more convenience to the crypto community, each innovation is a facility for you to manage your assets from the inside, it is a type of financial disruption that has important qualities to keep changing the world.

Decentralized finance is the main focus today, as it is a futuristic trend that is developing more and more strongly, reaching a level of consolidation that few thought possible, it is a balanced type of finance that acquires power as time goes by.

The skills to make a living from cryptocurrency trading

Making a living from cryptocurrency trading is a reality that more and more people are achieving, to the point of being the main source of income, but it is false that it is a simple and luxurious lifestyle in a short time, on the contrary, it requires a process of consolidation and constant income generation.

The standard of living is not exclusive, but covers all accounts, is part of one of the benefits of trading especially under its distance mode is conceived as an opportunity, but that average achievement is not easy or fleeting, it is all about a process that allows you to acquire the necessary skills to make a living from such activity.

Without certain specific trading skills it will not be possible to generate income that will provide you with security, the basic skills to make a living from cryptocurrency trading are the following:

- **Set a real goal**

The first thing is to establish a goal that is achievable, for this you just have to be honest or transparent with yourself, because as you know and take into account the self-control you have, you will be able to respond to some situations or doubts that may arise about this type of investment.

Normally you should clarify what trading does for you, also if you are looking to dedicate yourself to this profession full time and leave traditional work, once this is positive and negative, the next thing is to continue to create goals that are consistent, as it turns out to devote a daily learning time to trading.

In the midst of this training process, full commitment is required, without ceasing to read about this field or medium, whether about trading, cryptocurrencies and the market in general, these are bases of information from which you can not move away, the most advisable thing is that this does not decay above the profits obtained.

In addition, a good trading text can become your best ally, because it strengthens the level of psychology and allows you to design a strategy suited to your interests, this makes every novice, as well as experts as they are habits that you should not lose, learning is continuous, whether you see results or not this is the means to enhance your career.

For cryptocurrencies to be a profitable medium you must turn education into a consistent action, you must really like it so that you do the whole process with passion and do not depend only on the result, especially when it depends on a changing market because of the type of volatility, you can carry out these actions:

1. **Establish a plan and don't break it**

The design of a strategy is a commitment itself, but as in any investment you must try different modalities until you reach a definitive point, you may come across a better plan than another, but the essential thing is that you do not stick to any plan, that is, the first rule that you should not break is open experimentation.

You must stick to the plan of testing strategies, as well as being willing to change them, regardless of whether it was a good, bad or regular one, the important thing is to perform an analysis of each result, the intention is that you do not lose money without a legitimate reaction, so it is your duty to appeal to your discipline.

The will to stay on your feet in a volatile market requires that kind of focus, to stick to the letter of some strategy that is being accompanied by solid results, but it's all about getting that unique strategy that defines you, especially what makes this whole process easy for you.

Forming a trading plan is directly attached to your personality type, as well as the level of routine you are living, that way you can trade comfortably without a negative attachment, but a discipline faithful to the complications when they are plans that have generated you verifiable results, this is the way to reap profits.

2. **Manages capital and risk levels**

When you want to invest in cryptocurrency trading to make a living from it, you must set an amount of money, since this is what will allow you to operate and at the same time is the tool through which you will sustain the transactions, without the determination of the capital you will not be able to carry out any type of operation.

The work and management of cryptocurrencies is done based on your capital, and the next thing is to try to protect it at all costs, because as your capital is shortened you will not be able to stay alive in these investments, it is vital to take care of the steps you take and the risk you run, otherwise you can lapidate your first experiences.

There is only one way to succeed and come out unscathed in the markets, and the answer is based on earning income progressively, while managing risk every step of the way, keeping patience as the main resource.

At the beginning you can start earning only 0.5$ for each transaction, for example, in case of a day trading that develops approximately up to 5 or 8 transactions, but also within that measure you must accept that not all of them come out or end positively, and when you don't know a risk control method you can lose more than you earn.

But by mastering that level of risk awareness, you can open yourself up to another level of profit, especially when you bet on the use of 2% StopLoss, that kind of measure helps you not to lose more than 2% of what you have generated, this is important because you are always going to run into losing trades due to high volatility.

The percentage of people's profits must increase gradually, where it is key that the losses are not greater and above all that the capital can grow until a significant profit rate is built, since the money generated ends up attracting a higher percentage of money.

3. **Other recommendations to keep in mind**

Before you want to delve into the world of cryptocurrencies, you need to take into account that online they sell a totally wrong image of this medium, because they usually publish the positive factors of trading, causing more people to want to engage in this activity, but without delving into risk issues.

Trading and becoming a trader is not just a self-proclamation, to have investments that allow you to make a living from it you must do much more, so that the results of your operations are what define you, the rest is guesswork in this area, before any desire to operate you can consider these tips:

- Do not be in a hurry to become a successful investor in the world of cryptocurrencies, since that kind of haste does not leave good results, nor will it allow you to advance in a progressive environment, especially when you do not want to expose all your capital to these activities.
- You should only invest for those markets that you really know, and on which you are willing to lose, no matter if this is not the intention, there is no doubt that this is an outcome that you must deal with in order to become profitable.

- It is essential that you assume that being a trader demands to learn to live with some losses, no one is exempt from this type of results, it is a business where losing is possible and once you can assume it you can dare to keep learning and find the plan that best represents you.
- It is totally false that trading is about guessing the outcome of what is going to happen in any market, the trader is rather in charge of performing a function to take advantage of low prices or market movements, but for no reason is it a fortune teller or trying to fight with what the market imposes.
- There is no doubt that the key is in the type of training you receive, without forgetting to take steps that allow you to be closer to what happens in the market, this is called a preparation so that your account and your income will thank you.

The regular salary of the crypto world

One of the main portfolios of salaries or bonds today are cryptocurrencies, they are an optimal measure to build a way of living or carrying out expenses, to the point of creating a support for your retirements, all thanks to the decision to invest by these digital assets, even if they are the riskiest compared to other markets.

Building a wallet on the basis of cryptocurrencies is a full opportunity for your income to increase, for this you must reach a good month, for example, or what is equally translated as a period of good decisions, as it is the best way for your wallet to be strong.

The crucial goal in the cryptocurrency environment is to achieve stability, before starting you can bet on a progressive experiment, it is all about investing regularly on this asset, but you should know the following rules to follow nowadays:

- Invest through a confirmed option such as Binance, as it is one of the most stable markets worldwide and hosts a large number of cryptocurrencies.
- Each month you can dedicate an amount of around 60 euros to invest in cryptocurrencies, as one of the first steps to grow and start in this market without economic impediments.
- Invest half of the funds in stable and consolidated cryptocurrencies such as Bitcoin, for example, this works as a flying asset that can help you survive in this market.

- Beyond one stable currency, you can select three others, on which you can sustain an investment at least from the beginning until the end of that year.
- On the other hand, when you pay with cryptocurrencies you must visualize the deposits in Binance, that is the classification that this type of movement must have.
- At the end of a period of time you must decide if you can include other cryptocurrencies on the portfolio.
- The target or key point of this type of investment covers up to 10 years.

There is no doubt that investment in cryptocurrencies is a favorable option to think about retirement, since it provides excellent results to consider, this alternative allows to compensate the losses that are generated especially in the first month, even you are going to have the bonus of appealing for stable currencies.

The merits of each month are behind each success, one of the most promising bets today is Cardano, everything in general is a titanic work to find the best investment options, and then it is that you can measure the results to observe the increase each percentage.

The recording of the percentage gained allows you to control the psychological barrier, as you start to notice after each number that you are doing well, the impulse that you should not lose is to keep the margin of losses at bay, the results serve as an assessment to measure or change the cryptocurrency portfolio.

It is typical that you spend around 60 euros on some kind of purchase, when you can actually allocate this over a cryptocurrency wallet that can be more profitable for you, so the step to follow until they become a full habit is the following:

- **Cryptocurrency deposits**

It is common to want to freeze capital through cryptocurrencies, such deposits are known as an ideal way to reap interest, this is accrued to accumulate and have a type of subscription that is positioned automatically, so it is a continuous benefit.

The emphasis on this measure is that after a few months you can obtain important profits, since when your portfolio starts to work properly, you will find yourself with the type of income that will allow you to live better until your account balance reaches an optimal point.

Retirement savings in cryptocurrencies

Many countries in the world invest and adopt with greater confidence a fund destined for cryptocurrencies, this point is important to have liquidity in the future, this is due to the legal backing that some important assets such as Bitcoin have obtained, since that classifies it as a way of financial safeguard.

In the financial sector the place that cryptocurrencies occupy is a privilege, that is why even pension funds can be sustained thanks to this type of assets, where you can diversify the type of currencies that you include in your investment plan, it is a better offer for its amplitude compared to the traditional.

Most of the holdings are being declared in cryptocurrencies so that they do not lose their value as time goes by, most companies opt for this path of placing their assets on cryptocurrencies, to take advantage of the sustained increase in the value of each currency as an additional motive.

It is visible that you can generate important profits of the first level when detailing that your funds or capitals are on these digital currencies, in addition the handling of the money is simpler by means of this way, in the case of the Bitcoin for example it is an asset that possesses that reserve of value that the retirement requires.

Compared to a commodity this type of financial alternative has a better chance of surviving in the long term, because the investment earns interest and brings you happiness when there is an upward movement within the market, Bitcoin cannot be discounted because it has gained more margin than gold.

Instead of having only traditional assets such as bonds and stocks, cryptocurrencies are now incorporated, by building a portfolio it is possible to be part of the positive movements of the market, investments around this asset generate a highly favorable future scheme.

- **Speculation and the legitimate asset behind cryptocurrencies**

Beyond the satisfaction that investing in cryptocurrencies can generate, converting this currency into a pension fund can be risky, but at the same time it is a decision that generates better dividends, the acceptance of involving your funds in a speculative environment is a belief that must be adopted.

Bitcoin as a store of value may be overkill, especially since the price is volatile, but in the long run it is a solution to take into account, this just goes against some conservative stances, but it is still a trend to gain interest over any traditional pension fund.

Behind the behaviors related to this type of market, there is a very striking margin for big name companies that wish to be part of this medium, this type of utility over your pension fund has been chosen by Tesla, Square and many others.

Asset investment is a legitimization aid at the same time, as it is a highly mobile financial market not only in your home country, but on a global scale.

Buying cryptocurrencies as collateral on the road to retirement

Carrying out operations with Bitcoins, for example, can leave you in the next 10 years a significant retirement fund, therefore cryptocurrencies are recommended to exercise profitable investments, the option and the function of being a cryptocurrency trader is a must for you to have a much stronger future vision.

The optimism that exists about cryptocurrencies is anchored on its revaluation, it is the main reason why all types of investors dedicate their funds in cryptocurrencies, it is a viable way out especially to protect yourself against some specific economic situations that you are living.

Above some financial situations it also represents a great alternative to have your assets multiplied in the medium and long term, at the level of countries where their local currency is weak there is nothing like opting for some financial variations that are resistant as is the case of cryptocurrencies especially the stable ones.

The most advisable to start is to invest for a smaller amount on the most important cryptocurrencies, in case you are looking for a retirement measure you can opt for Bitcoin or Ethereum, but you should start by reducing minimal and unnecessary expenses to move on to invest those small amounts in cryptocurrencies to make it useful.

The intention of opting for a continuous revaluation of cryptocurrencies is a way to have forces or ways to respond in the future, the choice of large investors for this option is further evidence of the power of such digital assets, and their movements are those that generate pressure on the supply and price of such assets.

The valuation behind this type of assets is a parameter that you can use to decide, the development is clear, behind the name of each cryptocurrency there is a project that has a viable growth potential, this is an idea to deal with so that the assets you own can acquire another value as time goes by.

Retirement plans designed based on cryptocurrencies

Various reputable companies issue a retirement plan, within which bitcoin is widely used, and in this type of need some companies help and encourage the formation of a retirement plan with potential in exchange for payment to obtain their advice to secure your future.

Most of the portfolios created are guarded by the best plays, so that when an employee retires he/she can dispose of a whole fund that has generated interest for the time of his/her work, while the assets were allocated on those chosen assets that should contain potential for growth.

Currently there are more than 150 blockchain in Spain, and in each country that facilitate operations, allowing deposits to be feasible and then in the course of time you can, the adoption of this kind of technology allows companies to dedicate the pension fund in the plane of cryptocurrencies.

Similarly in China, Blockchain plans are designed on a daily basis to make every investment can go in escalation, and every area in Asia has become the epicenter of blockchain technology over other locations, this has to do with the promotion of this type of technology involved in different areas of society.

The immense technological development is part of the industrial innovation that is taking place in Asia, during the last 5 years it has strengthened and most of the local companies bet on this way to provide pension funds, which are sustained on the basis of the news arising from that environment.

- **Bitcoin and Ethereum can't miss on a retirement plan.**

Through the world of cryptocurrencies and all that it causes on a financial level, it is an exclusive opportunity so that through compounding you can be close to generating income, until you have liquidity to live comfortably, for this reason cryptoassets should be part of every retirement plan.

This type of betting on your future is part of a new order that overcomes centralization, this utility allows you to take advantage to exploit blockchain technology, as this medium represents a unique profitability contribution, especially because it allows diversification and is stronger compared to traditional media.

Having advice to create a retirement portfolio, increases the potential percentage that you will obtain an asset with a great future, when it comes to profitability this type of support is more reliable so that you do not have to take more risks, these instruments raise your profit percentages on the portfolio.

But in the midst of portfolio formation, there are other external details or elements, such as your age and goals, that count when setting up a plan that represents long-term gains, and by studying these details you can access an important source of profitability at high levels.

At a global level, it was traditionally invested in gold, silver and many other assets, but with the fall of its flow the arrival of cryptocurrencies took more strength, this new flow causes that pension care is invested to become a variable income, therefore it is a real alternative that makes sense.

The striking side of cryptocurrencies is the interest they generate, regardless of the level of risk that this option generates, so for those who are looking for diversification and profitability this alternative is the most appropriate because it meets these criteria, without underestimating the precautionary warnings.

This risk taking is a path that can enhance any kind of pension, up to the point of meeting the obligations and payments to be faced in the future, you should start by creating a profile to visualize the risk and the time to be faced until obtaining a variable income.

The special bet on Bitcoin is a special way for you to acquire an investment asset with a lot of future ahead, the important thing is that as you acquire more data you can continue to exercise analysis to adjust your investments towards market trends.

In the crypto-assets environment there is an important margin of capitalization, therefore it is an improvement of liquidity, for this reason a great amount of exchanges participate in the creation of pension funds, a contracting can be carried out to ensure your investment and you can have suitable assets.

There may still be a lot of criticism about this sector of the economy, but it is true that important assets such as Bitcoin impose a significant advance, but at the same time a lot of information has emerged that allows to trust this type of technology.

At the same time, some protocols have been imposed so that the ability to carry out some contracts is not diminished, so you can get a basic learning that allows you to bet on the asset you want especially to get some profits from this liquid and updated market.

The important thing is to ask yourself the question if you are able to measure and hold a position that is not so speculative, but with a long term plan that is built with solid positions of high projections, this is achieved as you are able to exercise a thorough vision of each asset.

The views to consider to take advantage of cryptocurrencies, is the one that allows you to operate and make decisions on your own, that kind of management is a personal issue, but you can use some digital wallets where you can apply some techniques that are related to obtaining passive income.

Depending on each investor you can choose the disposition of your capital, to begin with, proliferate the type of opportunities you possess, this new industry is at your vision, it all depends on your goals and around it is that you are going to build the retirement plan.

- **The futuristic estimate of a pension plan**

A prioritized attention must be dedicated on the future that the pension plan has, with that kind of futuristic vision a cryptocurrency investment is built, this sophisticated aspect is what you require because to reach some level of return, you can draw and study data on profitability, risk and other factors.

Following this path allows you to obtain a balanced portfolio, taking into account the measures of profitability and risk, by understanding this you can visualize the ups and downs without so much fear in between, the limitations can be placed by yourself until you are as conservative as you wish, the essential thing is that your pension fund is protected.

In this way you can elaborate an efficient plan, but the combination of assets is always conceived as an optimal modality to take care of yourself, in this way you will find yourself with striking and clear data, the important thing is that everything is well distributed to achieve a variable income, in this way the composition will be effective.

The special reading is what allows you to compare data, with which your funds can cause pensions to be much more useful, in view of the characteristics of the assets that make up the same, as there are movements will be results that affect your current pension plans.

The level of risk provided by cryptocurrencies is a way to raise profitability, but through a bet where the technological side acquires more strength, the willingness to have digital money is a current power to use assets that gather a lot of characteristics to make them ideal investment assets.

To trade with this type of assets, you must have the clear idea of living with some bitter moments, it is part of the good and not so good side that will accompany you until you decide to withdraw all the funds dedicated to such pension plan, using to the maximum the value and potential of cryptocurrencies.

Launching Bitwage to create a retirement plan

The options available in the market are extended through Bitwage, where the opportunity arises to be part of the first BTC 401(k) around the world, this is part of a retirement plan to which they can have access, this project is accompanied by part of the partnership of Gemini and Kingdom Trust.

Each employee who is enrolled has the ability to invest in two modes, first, of traditional Roth 401(k) type dollars, all of this comes from the service provider that has Bitwage payrolls, where a Bitcoin 401(k) plan has been designed.

These types of examples demonstrate the acceptance that cryptocurrencies are having, these plans are accepted and designed by a large number of companies and companies, one of them is Gemini and it all started through a test of at least 10 months of duration so that each employee began to invest in Bitcoin.

- **What a 401(k) plan represents**

A large number of companies are sponsoring the practice and preference on a special savings plan to cover dedicated retirements for their employees, by building these plans you can secure your future, they are also known as defined contribution plans.

This option allows you to easily save money to take control of your retirement, without the need to worry about federal taxes, much less state taxes, it is an income on your funds until you are able to withdraw the total fund at retirement, and this is one of the most common plans.

- **Retirement through Bitcoin**

Bitwage trading with Gemini provides the opportunity to create a pension plan, this is possible or real by means of exchanges platforms of maximum confidence not to run any kind of risk, in addition everything is developed by means of a type of custody imposed by the best and possesses administration function.

The demographic profile imposed by each company, allows to adapt to the type of cryptocurrencies that is convenient to buy, for this a navigation is made to take advantage of the most opportune economic times, this is favorable for companies to reduce payroll expenses that involves or has to do with retirement.

These plans provide the opportunity to create contributions to create benefits through 401(k) accounts, and for employees it means getting much more, through an innovative way you can turn your investment into a larger number than what was introduced at the beginning.

- **Training and securing your future after investments**

In the specific case of Bitwage, plans are being developed that in the future originate visible advantages, it is the best compared to other financial products, this becomes a reality under a solid plan such as the 401(k), it is an alternative for traders to monitor the fund destined for their retirement.

In the future these types of plans are going to allow more cryptocurrencies to be used, but for now everything is betting on the stability of Bitcoin, in the case of this plan it was designed since 2014 and since then it has been the most dominant modality to keep a payroll alive so that payments can be issued in Ethereum, Bitcoin, and much more.

This type of company also has as a project or main purpose that freelancers can have their payments in cryptocurrencies, since they provide this service for Upwork and also for Toptal, making digital currencies more valid than ever and an ideal exchange of value.

Even in inheritance plans the cryptocurrency path is being used frequently, especially in regions where it is very expensive to maintain this type of services or calculations, without the value of the properties being at risk, this path is feasible over different areas that is why they are plans that are revolutionizing everything.

The best cryptocurrencies for creating a pension plan

As you near middle age it is common to think about your comforts and guarantees, so to live retirement to the fullest you can consider some forms of investment that take care of your long-term wealth without being a headache, by making positive decisions you can be a lucky one and have regular income.

When you have a job you earn a salary, which must be a link to obtain a decent pension that allows you to live fully, this is difficult to achieve in this type of current economic situation or global crises, and one way to secure your assets is through cryptocurrencies to have a useful income.

In the face of the State's inaction to care for and build your pension plan, an independent and private option allows you to acquire marvelous percentages to live better when you reach retirement, but you should not opt for banking but rather for a decentralized means that generates more freedoms for you.

Investment in cryptocurrencies is interesting to obtain outstanding benefits, beyond the fact that it is an uncertain or uncontrollable alternative, but the truth is that it facilitates the creation of a pension plan towards a different result from the other options and above all it is more profitable, to the point of knowing and participating more actively with your funds.

There is no comparison on the level of profitability that cryptocurrencies have, where the representation of Bitcoin stands out, because an investment that you make today, can be transformed into a double or triple measure, making any investment plan profitable.

But it's not all about cryptocurrencies, you can diversify assets towards other cryptocurrencies that are promising in the long term, at the moment you can opt for Monero and Faircoin, as they are options that you can exploit to secure your pension, but equally you can place your trust on other options.

Normally you can closely follow the development of Litecoin, Ethereum, Dash and many more of this type, the essential thing is to form a portfolio suitable in every way so that when retirement presents itself you have ways to respond to the various commitments you are about to face without thinking about money or inactivity.

Cryptoassets as a sign of the future for pension funds

All that cryptoassets represent translates into a clear hope to make pension funds worthwhile, completely displacing the role of traditional financial institutions, this solution is a movement of confidence to multiply your funds, beyond the changes that are visualized in the market.

Before some bearish windows it is a formidable entry so that your capital can increase, since you would be buying cryptocurrencies at a low price, so that each rise can be used as a personal gain after each percentage increase of the original value, therefore an important collection can be produced for you.

A lot of companies are able to provide a hedge fund for pensions concentrated in cryptocurrencies, where it is possible to have access to a fuller administration, the crucial thing is not behind the capital but the interest generated, since that is what sustains your pension fund.

Once there are some highs in the market, you can get good news, but as an investor you need to remain cautious especially when closely watching the changes in the capital, which must be preserved under a bearish facet so as not to burn its value.

Funds dedicated to cryptocurrencies are a solution and at the same time a challenge, because at the level of details it is a complicated picture as every level of trading affects the price of assets, but working and associating pension funds with cryptocurrencies is not a fact that happens out of the blue.

An ancillary measure is pension investment fund managers, in the end digital assets provide convenience, education is required and a large amount of time invested, thus the advantages and disadvantages can be analyzed, up to follow the steps of the chief investment officers.

The main and only obstacle to put your assets in the hands of cryptocurrencies is the degree of volatility, but each movement or variant must be accepted by a high dose of patience, these are key factors to venture into the future of this type of market as changing as it is cryptocurrencies.

A large number of investors become attached and familiar with digital assets, they are the ones that generate comfort for the control that can be exercised over your funds, which causes that while capital is inserted, greater are the benefits when the right paths are followed.

The victory that can be reaped on digital asset funds is a guarantee that they will not devalue, which is useful in retirement matters, cryptocurrencies may be volatile, but they meet the criteria of having a better evolution compared to traditional financial products.

The performance of cryptocurrencies is asymmetric, which implies that the upside potential you may encounter is higher than the downside potential, and within this behavior Bitcoin meets this measure of return, it is the key pillar to carry out an institutional investment.

The vision of investing a fund on a cryptocurrency is a task or an encouraging step because of the margin of growth, as long as all the associated risks are accepted naturally, you will be able to manage the capital in a better way, it is a smart way to escape inflation and just deal with acceptable risks of a market.

Some investment movements suffer in the face of speculation, this becomes one of the most tense moments, as certain movements can completely disconcert you, but it all depends on the duration of the bear market as well as the volatility that is occurring on cryptocurrencies.

The beneficiaries of such a fund require a maximum level of research, so that from the launch of the investment your money begins to confront risks, but an investment team stays on top of the picture regardless of any concerns you may have.

More and more backgrounds are being marked in cryptocurrency investment to live fully in the future, where each participant begins to wonder on what digital assets it will be convenient to place their funds so that in the coming years the interests begin to emerge.

Actions to avoid in order to make a living from cryptocurrencies

Regardless of the type of cryptocurrency you prefer or the one you are investing in, there are some precautions or recommendations to take seriously, as this will allow you to achieve the financial freedom you long for, but it is a field where reading is everything, especially within the market behavior.

1. Lack of knowledge about cryptocurrency

What you should not forget is that this is an activity that can generate significant losses, but the concentration should be all the time on what you can win, instead of being pessimistic because that only violates your emotional side, so an action to avoid is the ignorance of what you invest.

Behind every type of cryptocurrency there is a purpose, by knowing these points you can follow the news of such sector especially based on blockchain technology where many data circulate that are not fully understood, but provide you with a clear advantage.

In a broad way this helps you to recognize the quotation that exists on it, that is to say the amount of purchases and sales in between, all this can be known through the information or statistics that an Exchange has, the same happens with handling a great amount of information about the wallet that you are going to use.

It recognizes first and foremost that this type of digital asset is fully decentralized, and the predictions about it is positioned as a mainstay of the economy of the future, which is why pensions revolve around this asset class, which is why they are most often used as an investment rather than a form of payment.

2. **Read and follow any site found online**

When it comes to your assets you can't trust just anyone, especially because you can be a victim of scams or participate in a fund that is involved in corruption, so one way to learn is through expert advice, as well as your own mistakes by starting a 100% legal registration on your own.

Behind every decision is the future of your money, opting for cryptocurrencies is not a light step, for any reason it is not healthy to act in a hurry, sometimes following impulses does not bring you any positive result, so it is better to prefer a more secure and explicit way.

Instead of believing everything you read, it is best to refer to official sources, without forgetting that you should not share your financial information even with acquaintances, since the control of digital assets depends on the kind of care you can exercise from the beginning.

3. **Spending a fortune on courses with no reputation**

Learning to invest in cryptocurrencies is not easy, much less if you want these assets can represent your funds in the future, so it is not enough with some lectures or much less, it is best to engage fully to clear any doubts, without wasting too much time in just practice because you miss opportunities.

In the market there are some gaps that you should not miss, but learning is vital so the most appropriate thing to do is not to waste time but to dedicate yourself to analyze your options, without the need to take impulsive actions that are responsible for making the investment for you, it is a matter of following what is more professional and effective.

What cannot be avoided is the duty to learn, but neither can it be taken to the extreme of being part of a course whose only objective is to extract your money, since they will only give you advice that sounds nice, but in the development of the market it will not generate any effect, much less prepare your psychology.

4. Choosing a cryptocurrency for a bullish promise

Thinking about making a living from cryptocurrencies and getting easy money is not something that happens overnight, so above greed you must understand that some cryptocurrencies receive advertising to benefit those who are already inside, plus you require guidance to identify the fall of that peak or bullish moment.

In the market the common pattern is that there is a high price level, and then a downward trend, it is part of the dynamics of this type of environment, because as in any other investment everything that goes up has to go down, throughout history such patterns are part of any economy.

It is usual that you hear or read many publications where they recommend you to buy because they will be worth a lot in the future, this type of concept is established on most of the assets.

The important thing is that you are able to recognize its value, as well as determine whether it has the potential to escalate in price, since the future cannot be read, but at present you can measure what the cryptocurrency is for, it is a preview of how far it is capable of going, since no price is stable at all.

The seasons and news affect a price, so the real value is relative and it is difficult to determine with certainty any projection, but when it comes to living from this activity the most appropriate is to bet on the assets that are more stable so you can rely on it for your retirement.

5. **Borrowing and raising your expenses by investing in cryptocurrencies**

Investing in cryptocurrencies as a lifestyle, goes hand in hand with a decrease in your expenses, unless your earnings are above the consumption you make, this helps your funds as a whole can earn interest without hardship, also the capital involved on the cryptocurrency should be a fund that you do not need.

In the case of pensions and retirement, it has to do with the administration and protection of the funds, as a useful measure in the face of inflation as well as the intervention and commissions generated by public institutions, which, in addition to everything else, do not generate any type of capital increase.

When you want to make a living from these digital assets, you should not consider earning too much or wanting to recover with someone else's money, as that would be extreme pressure when the results you are looking for are not produced, this giant problem does not allow you to see the opportunities, without leaving aside that you can get into debt.

This type of action of borrowing only makes everything worse, the most usual are testimonials in which a whole family sells its wealth to invest it in cryptocurrency, which is more sensible than borrowing, although it is observed in a different way, in the long term it generates more opportunities a strong capital based on your wealth.

Instead of looking at investments as an impossible event, you can start by allocating your junk food expenses or just a few $5 a month, weekly or however you prefer, can be directed towards building a cryptocurrency fund that can represent you tomorrow.

6. **Betting on cryptocurrencies with a poor track record**

Living on the income and movements of cryptocurrencies depends mostly on choosing stable assets, especially when you want to spend your retirement on these currencies, because if you have a solid project and a scalable behavior behind it, you can become a millionaire in the long run or your funds will have acquired important interests.

This applies to all cryptocurrencies in general, since opting for those worth $1 today, only to expect massive growth in a few years to have a price of $100 or more, is a futuristic measure, but at the same time empty, since there are many factors involved to certify that it is a cryptocurrency with potential.

Finding such opportunities is complicated, in any case depends on the vision and study of experts who measure emerging cryptocurrencies, but nothing is written in this type of market, the idea of multiplying your money in this world is a progressive escalation, the essential thing is not to buy or invest everything without having a research base.